Artificial Harmonics

for the Cello

Book One

by Cassia Harvey

CHP145

©2005 by C. Harvey Publications All Rights Reserved.

www.charveypublications.com - print books & free sheet music blog
www.learnstrings.com - PDF downloadable books & chamber music

Artificial Harmonics for the Cello, Book One

1

Cassia Harvey

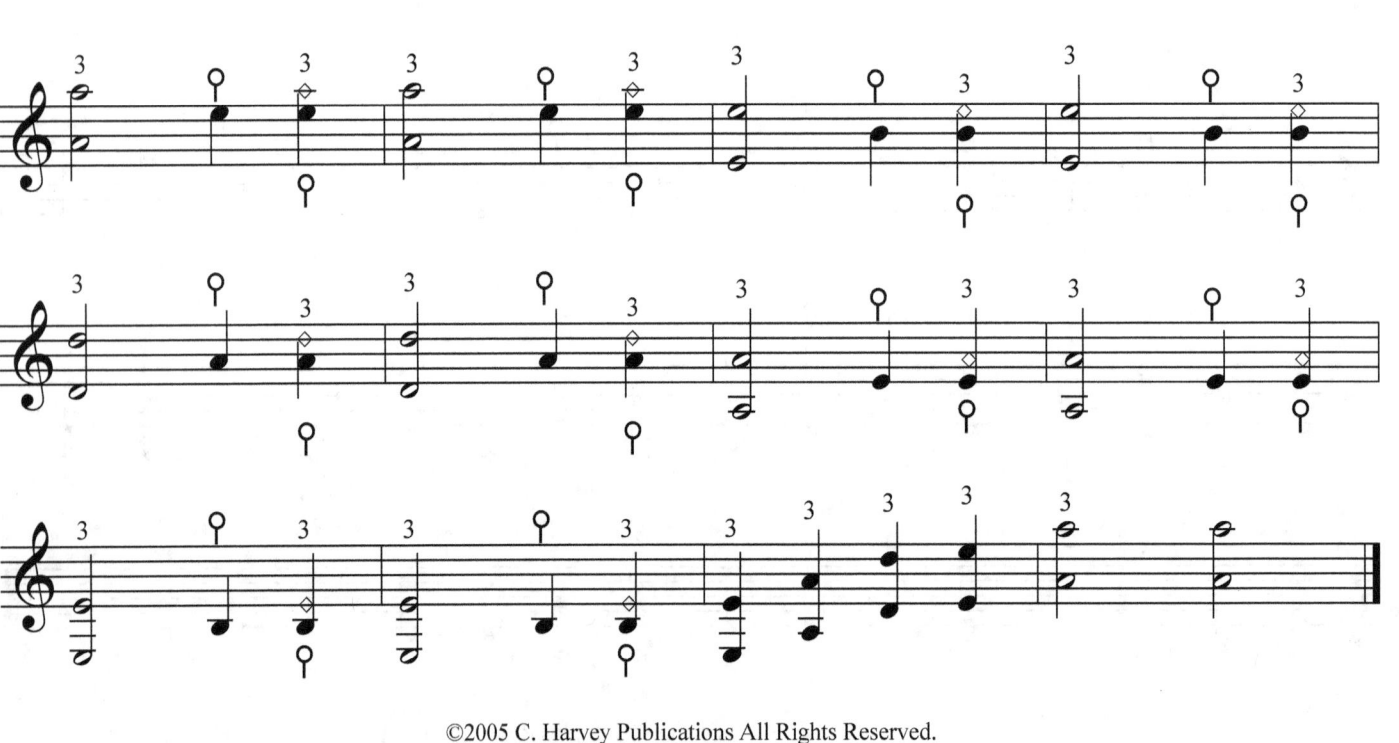

3

4

5

6

7

8

Artificial Harmonics for the Cello, Book One

9

©2005 C. Harvey Publications All Rights Reserved.

10

11

12

13

14

15

16

17

18

19

20

21

22

23

24

25

26

27

28

29

31

32

33

www.ingramcontent.com/pod-product-compliance
Lightning Source LLC
Chambersburg PA
CBHW051427070526
44584CB00023B/3616